Welcome!

Please sign our guest book

Name(s): _____

Date of my/our visit: _____

I/we traveled from: _____

Highlights of my/our stay

_____

_____

_____

Places I / we recommend

_____

_____

_____

_____

Message to the host

_____

_____

_____

_____

Name(s): ---

Date of my/our visit: --

I/we traveled from: --

Highlights of my/our stay

Places I / we recommend

Message to the host

Name(s): --

Date of my/our visit: --

I/we traveled from: --

Highlights of my/our stay

Places I / we recommend

Message to the host

Name(s): --

Date of my/our visit: --

I/we traveled from: ---

Highlights of my/our stay

Places I / we recommend

Message to the host

Name(s): _____

Date of my/our visit: _____

I/we traveled from: _____

Highlights of my/our stay

_____

_____

_____

Places I / we recommend

_____

_____

_____

_____

Message to the host

_____

_____

_____

_____

Name(s): _____

Date of my/our visit: _____

I/we traveled from: _____

Highlights of my/our stay

_____

_____

_____

Places I / we recommend

_____

_____

_____

_____

Message to the host

_____

_____

_____

_____

Name(s): _____

Date of my/our visit: _____

I/we traveled from: _____

Highlights of my/our stay

_____

_____

_____

Places I / we recommend

_____

_____

_____

_____

Message to the host

_____

_____

_____

_____

Name(s): --

Date of my/our visit: --

I/we traveled from: ---

Highlights of my/our stay

Places I / we recommend

Message to the host

Name(s): _____

Date of my/our visit: _____

I/we traveled from: _____

Highlights of my/our stay

_____

_____

_____

Places I / we recommend

_____

_____

_____

_____

Message to the host

_____

_____

_____

Name(s): _____

Date of my/our visit: _____

I/we traveled from: _____

Highlights of my/our stay

_____

_____

_____

Places I / we recommend

_____

_____

_____

Message to the host

_____

_____

_____

_____

Name(s):

Date of my/our visit:

I/we traveled from:

Highlights of my/our stay

Places I / we recommend

Message to the host

Name(s): _____

Date of my/our visit: _____

I/we traveled from: _____

Highlights of my/our stay

_____

_____

_____

Places I / we recommend

_____

_____

_____

_____

Message to the host

_____

_____

_____

_____

Name(s): _____

Date of my/our visit: _____

I/we traveled from: _____

Highlights of my/our stay

_____

_____

_____

Places I / we recommend

_____

_____

_____

_____

Message to the host

_____

_____

_____

_____

Name(s): _____

Date of my/our visit: _____

I/we traveled from: _____

Highlights of my/our stay

_____

_____

_____

Places I / we recommend

_____

_____

_____

_____

Message to the host

_____

_____

_____

_____

Name(s): _____

Date of my/our visit: _____

I/we traveled from: _____

Highlights of my/our stay

_____

_____

_____

Places I / we recommend

_____

_____

_____

Message to the host

_____

_____

_____

Name(s): _____

Date of my/our visit: _____

I/we traveled from: _____

Highlights of my/our stay

_____
_____
_____

Places I / we recommend

_____
_____
_____
_____

Message to the host

_____
_____
_____
_____

Name(s): _____

Date of my/our visit: _____

I/we traveled from: _____

Highlights of my/our stay

_____

_____

_____

Places I / we recommend

_____

_____

_____

_____

Message to the host

_____

_____

_____

_____

Name(s): --

Date of my/our visit: --

I/we traveled from: --

Highlights of my/our stay

Places I / we recommend

Message to the host

Name(s): _____

Date of my/our visit: _____

I/we traveled from: _____

Highlights of my/our stay

_____

_____

_____

Places I / we recommend

_____

_____

_____

_____

Message to the host

_____

_____

_____

_____

Name(s): ---

Date of my/our visit: ---

I/we traveled from: ---

Highlights of my/our stay

Places I / we recommend

Message to the host

Name(s): _____

Date of my/our visit: _____

I/we traveled from: _____

Highlights of my/our stay

_____

_____

_____

Places I / we recommend

_____

_____

_____

_____

Message to the host

_____

_____

_____

_____

Name(s): --

Date of my/our visit: --------------------------------

I/we traveled from: -----------------------------------

Highlights of my/our stay

Places I / we recommend

Message to the host

Name(s): _____

Date of my/our visit: _____

I/we traveled from: _____

Highlights of my/our stay

_____

_____

_____

Places I / we recommend

_____

_____

_____

_____

Message to the host

_____

_____

_____

Name(s): _____

Date of my/our visit: _____

I/we traveled from: _____

Highlights of my/our stay

_____

_____

_____

Places I / we recommend

_____

_____

_____

Message to the host

_____

_____

_____

_____

Name(s): _____

Date of my/our visit: _____

I/we traveled from: _____

Highlights of my/our stay

_____

_____

_____

Places I / we recommend

_____

_____

_____

_____

Message to the host

_____

_____

_____

_____

Name(s): --

Date of my/our visit: --

I/we traveled from: ---

Highlights of my/our stay

Places I / we recommend

Message to the host

Name(s): --

Date of my/our visit: --

I/we traveled from: --

Highlights of my/our stay

Places I / we recommend

Message to the host

Name(s): ---

Date of my/our visit: ---

I/we traveled from: ---

Highlights of my/our stay

Places I / we recommend

Message to the host

Name(s): --

Date of my/our visit: --

I/we traveled from: --

Highlights of my/our stay

Places I / we recommend

Message to the host

Name(s): _____

Date of my/our visit: _____

I/we traveled from: _____

Highlights of my/our stay

_____
_____
_____

Places I / we recommend

_____
_____
_____
_____

Message to the host

_____
_____
_____
_____

Name(s): _____

Date of my/our visit: _____

I/we traveled from: _____

Highlights of my/our stay

_____

_____

_____

Places I / we recommend

_____

_____

_____

_____

Message to the host

_____

_____

_____

_____

Name(s): --

Date of my/our visit: ------------------------------------

I/we traveled from: --------------------------------------

Highlights of my/our stay

Places I / we recommend

Message to the host

Name(s): _____

Date of my/our visit: _____

I/we traveled from: _____

Highlights of my/our stay

_____

_____

_____

Places I / we recommend

_____

_____

_____

_____

Message to the host

_____

_____

_____

Name(s): ---

Date of my/our visit: ---

I/we traveled from: ---

Highlights of my/our stay

Places I / we recommend

Message to the host

Name(s): --

Date of my/our visit: --

I/we traveled from: --

Highlights of my/our stay

Places I / we recommend

Message to the host

Name(s): _____

Date of my/our visit: _____

I/we traveled from: _____

✦✦✦✦✦

Highlights of my/our stay

_____

_____

_____

✦✦✦✦✦

Places I / we recommend

_____

_____

_____

_____

✦✦✦✦✦

Message to the host

_____

_____

_____

_____

Name(s): _____

Date of my/our visit: _____

I/we traveled from: _____

Highlights of my/our stay

_____

_____

_____

Places I / we recommend

_____

_____

_____

_____

Message to the host

_____

_____

_____

_____

Name(s):

Date of my/our visit:

I/we traveled from:

Highlights of my/our stay

Places I / we recommend

Message to the host

Name(s): _____

Date of my/our visit: _____

I/we traveled from: _____

Highlights of my/our stay

_____

_____

_____

Places I / we recommend

_____

_____

_____

_____

Message to the host

_____

_____

_____

_____

Name(s): _____

Date of my/our visit: _____

I/we traveled from: _____

Highlights of my/our stay

_____

_____

_____

Places I / we recommend

_____

_____

_____

_____

Message to the host

_____

_____

_____

_____

Name(s): _____

Date of my/our visit: _____

I/we traveled from: _____

Highlights of my/our stay

_____

_____

_____

Places I / we recommend

_____

_____

_____

_____

Message to the host

_____

_____

_____

_____

Name(s): --

Date of my/our visit: ---

I/we traveled from: --

Highlights of my/our stay

Places I / we recommend

Message to the host

Name(s): _____

Date of my/our visit: _____

I/we traveled from: _____

Highlights of my/our stay

_____

_____

_____

Places I / we recommend

_____

_____

_____

Message to the host

_____

_____

_____

Name(s): ....

Date of my/our visit: ....

I/we traveled from: ....

Highlights of my/our stay

....

....

....

Places I / we recommend

....

....

....

....

Message to the host

....

....

....

....

Name(s): _____

Date of my/our visit: _____

I/we traveled from: _____

Highlights of my/our stay

_____

_____

_____

Places I / we recommend

_____

_____

_____

_____

Message to the host

_____

_____

_____

_____

Name(s): --

Date of my/our visit: --

I/we traveled from: ---

Highlights of my/our stay

Places I / we recommend

Message to the host

Name(s):

Date of my/our visit:

I/we traveled from:

Highlights of my/our stay

Places I / we recommend

Message to the host

Name(s): ---

Date of my/our visit: --

I/we traveled from: --

Highlights of my/our stay

Places I / we recommend

Message to the host

Name(s): --

Date of my/our visit: --

I/we traveled from: --

Highlights of my/our stay

Places I / we recommend

Message to the host

Name(s): _____

Date of my/our visit: _____

I/we traveled from: _____

Highlights of my/our stay

_____

_____

_____

Places I / we recommend

_____

_____

_____

_____

Message to the host

_____

_____

_____

Name(s): _____

Date of my/our visit: _____

I/we traveled from: _____

Highlights of my/our stay

_____

_____

_____

Places I / we recommend

_____

_____

_____

_____

Message to the host

_____

_____

_____

_____

Name(s): --

Date of my/our visit: --

I/we traveled from: ---

Highlights of my/our stay

Places I / we recommend

Message to the host

Name(s): _____

Date of my/our visit: _____

I/we traveled from: _____

Highlights of my/our stay

_____

_____

_____

Places I / we recommend

_____

_____

_____

_____

Message to the host

_____

_____

_____

Name(s): --

Date of my/our visit: --

I/we traveled from: --

Highlights of my/our stay

Places I / we recommend

Message to the host

Name(s): --

Date of my/our visit: ---

I/we traveled from: --

Highlights of my/our stay

Places I / we recommend

Message to the host

Name(s): --

Date of my/our visit: --

I/we traveled from: ---

Highlights of my/our stay

Places I / we recommend

Message to the host

Name(s): _____

Date of my/our visit: _____

I/we traveled from: _____

Highlights of my/our stay

_____

_____

_____

Places I / we recommend

_____

_____

_____

_____

Message to the host

_____

_____

_____

_____

Name(s): --

Date of my/our visit: --

I/we traveled from: --

Highlights of my/our stay

Places I / we recommend

Message to the host

Name(s): _____

Date of my/our visit: _____

I/we traveled from: _____

--- ❧ ---

Highlights of my/our stay

_____

_____

_____

--- ❧ ---

Places I / we recommend

_____

_____

_____

_____

--- ❧ ---

Message to the host

_____

_____

_____

_____

Name(s): --

Date of my/our visit: --

I/we traveled from: --

Highlights of my/our stay

Places I / we recommend

Message to the host

Name(s): ---

Date of my/our visit: --

I/we traveled from: --

Highlights of my/our stay

Places I / we recommend

Message to the host

Name(s): _____

Date of my/our visit: _____

I/we traveled from: _____

Highlights of my/our stay

_____

_____

_____

Places I / we recommend

_____

_____

_____

_____

Message to the host

_____

_____

_____

_____

Name(s): _____

Date of my/our visit: _____

I/we traveled from: _____

Highlights of my/our stay

_____

_____

_____

Places I / we recommend

_____

_____

_____

Message to the host

_____

_____

_____

Name(s): ---

Date of my/our visit: --

I/we traveled from: --

Highlights of my/our stay

Places I / we recommend

Message to the host

Name(s): _____

Date of my/our visit: _____

I/we traveled from: _____

Highlights of my/our stay

_____
_____
_____

Places I / we recommend

_____
_____
_____
_____

Message to the host

_____
_____
_____
_____

Name(s): _____

Date of my/our visit: _____

I/we traveled from: _____

Highlights of my/our stay

_____

_____

_____

Places I / we recommend

_____

_____

_____

_____

Message to the host

_____

_____

_____

_____

Name(s): _____

Date of my/our visit: _____

I/we traveled from: _____

Highlights of my/our stay

_____

_____

_____

Places I / we recommend

_____

_____

_____

_____

Message to the host

_____

_____

_____

_____

Name(s): --

Date of my/our visit: --

I/we traveled from: --

Highlights of my/our stay

Places I / we recommend

Message to the host

Name(s):

Date of my/our visit:

I/we traveled from:

Highlights of my/our stay

Places I / we recommend

Message to the host

Name(s): ---

Date of my/our visit: ---

I/we traveled from: --

Highlights of my/our stay

Places I / we recommend

Message to the host

Name(s): _____

Date of my/our visit: _____

I/we traveled from: _____

Highlights of my/our stay

_____

_____

_____

Places I / we recommend

_____

_____

_____

_____

Message to the host

_____

_____

_____

_____

Name(s): _____

Date of my/our visit: _____

I/we traveled from: _____

Highlights of my/our stay

_____

_____

_____

Places I / we recommend

_____

_____

_____

_____

Message to the host

_____

_____

_____

_____

Name(s): _____

Date of my/our visit: _____

I/we traveled from: _____

Highlights of my/our stay

_____
_____
_____

Places I / we recommend

_____
_____
_____
_____

Message to the host

_____
_____
_____
_____

Name(s):

Date of my/our visit:

I/we traveled from:

Highlights of my/our stay

Places I / we recommend

Message to the host

Name(s): _____

Date of my/our visit: _____

I/we traveled from: _____

Highlights of my/our stay

_____

_____

_____

Places I / we recommend

_____

_____

_____

Message to the host

_____

_____

_____

Name(s): ---

Date of my/our visit: --

I/we traveled from: ---

Highlights of my/our stay

Places I / we recommend

Message to the host

Name(s): _____

Date of my/our visit: _____

I/we traveled from: _____

Highlights of my/our stay

_____

_____

_____

Places I / we recommend

_____

_____

_____

_____

Message to the host

_____

_____

_____

_____

Name(s): --

Date of my/our visit: --

I/we traveled from: ---

Highlights of my/our stay

Places I / we recommend

Message to the host

Name(s): _____

Date of my/our visit: _____

I/we traveled from: _____

Highlights of my/our stay

_____

_____

_____

Places I / we recommend

_____

_____

_____

_____

Message to the host

_____

_____

_____

_____

Name(s): ---

Date of my/our visit: ---

I/we traveled from: ---

Highlights of my/our stay

Places I / we recommend

Message to the host

Name(s): _____

Date of my/our visit: _____

I/we traveled from: _____

Highlights of my/our stay

_____

_____

_____

Places I / we recommend

_____

_____

_____

_____

Message to the host

_____

_____

_____

_____

Name(s): --

Date of my/our visit: --

I/we traveled from: --

Highlights of my/our stay

Places I / we recommend

Message to the host

Name(s): _____

Date of my/our visit: _____

I/we traveled from: _____

Highlights of my/our stay

_____

_____

_____

Places I / we recommend

_____

_____

_____

_____

Message to the host

_____

_____

_____

Name(s):

Date of my/our visit:

I/we traveled from:

Highlights of my/our stay

Places I / we recommend

Message to the host

Name(s): --

Date of my/our visit: --

I/we traveled from: --

Highlights of my/our stay

Places I / we recommend

Message to the host

Name(s): ---

Date of my/our visit: ---

I/we traveled from: ---

Highlights of my/our stay

Places I / we recommend

Message to the host

Name(s): --

Date of my/our visit: --

I/we traveled from: --

Highlights of my/our stay

Places I / we recommend

Message to the host

Name(s): _____

Date of my/our visit: _____

I/we traveled from: _____

Highlights of my/our stay

_____

_____

_____

Places I / we recommend

_____

_____

_____

_____

Message to the host

_____

_____

_____

_____

Name(s): _____

Date of my/our visit: _____

I/we traveled from: _____

Highlights of my/our stay

_____

_____

_____

Places I / we recommend

_____

_____

_____

_____

Message to the host

_____

_____

_____

_____

Name(s): --

Date of my/our visit: --

I/we traveled from: ---

Highlights of my/our stay

Places I / we recommend

Message to the host

Name(s): _____

Date of my/our visit: _____

I/we traveled from: _____

✦ ✦ ✦

Highlights of my/our stay

_____

_____

_____

✦ ✦ ✦

Places I / we recommend

_____

_____

_____

_____

✦ ✦ ✦

Message to the host

_____

_____

_____

_____

Name(s):

Date of my/our visit:

I/we traveled from:

Highlights of my/our stay

Places I / we recommend

Message to the host

Name(s): _____

Date of my/our visit: _____

I/we traveled from: _____

Highlights of my/our stay

_____

_____

_____

Places I / we recommend

_____

_____

_____

_____

Message to the host

_____

_____

_____

_____

Name(s): --

Date of my/our visit: --

I/we traveled from: --

Highlights of my/our stay

Places I / we recommend

Message to the host

Name(s): _____

Date of my/our visit: _____

I/we traveled from: _____

Highlights of my/our stay

_____

_____

_____

Places I / we recommend

_____

_____

_____

_____

Message to the host

_____

_____

_____

Name(s): _____

Date of my/our visit: _____

I/we traveled from: _____

Highlights of my/our stay

_____

_____

_____

Places I / we recommend

_____

_____

_____

_____

Message to the host

_____

_____

_____

_____

Name(s): --

Date of my/our visit: --

I/we traveled from: ---

Highlights of my/our stay

Places I / we recommend

Message to the host

Name(s): --

Date of my/our visit: --

I/we traveled from: ---

Highlights of my/our stay

Places I / we recommend

Message to the host

Name(s): _____

Date of my/our visit: _____

I/we traveled from: _____

Highlights of my/our stay

_____

_____

_____

Places I / we recommend

_____

_____

_____

_____

Message to the host

_____

_____

_____

_____

Name(s): _____

Date of my/our visit: _____

I/we traveled from: _____

Highlights of my/our stay

_____

_____

_____

Places I / we recommend

_____

_____

_____

_____

Message to the host

_____

_____

_____

_____

Name(s): _____

Date of my/our visit: _____

I/we traveled from: _____

Highlights of my/our stay

_____

_____

_____

Places I / we recommend

_____

_____

_____

Message to the host

_____

_____

_____

Name(s):

Date of my/our visit:

I/we traveled from:

Highlights of my/our stay

Places I / we recommend

Message to the host

Name(s): _____

Date of my/our visit: _____

I/we traveled from: _____

Highlights of my/our stay

_____

_____

_____

Places I / we recommend

_____

_____

_____

_____

Message to the host

_____

_____

_____

Name(s): _____

Date of my/our visit: _____

I/we traveled from: _____

Highlights of my/our stay

_____

_____

_____

Places I / we recommend

_____

_____

_____

_____

Message to the host

_____

_____

_____

_____

Name(s): _____

Date of my/our visit: _____

I/we traveled from: _____

Highlights of my/our stay

_____

_____

_____

Places I / we recommend

_____

_____

_____

Message to the host

_____

_____

_____

Name(s): --

Date of my/our visit: --

I/we traveled from: --

❧ ━━━━━━━━━❧❦❧━━━━━━━━━ ❧

Highlights of my/our stay

❧ ━━━━━━━━━❧❦❧━━━━━━━━━ ❧

Places I / we recommend

❧ ━━━━━━━━━❧❦❧━━━━━━━━━ ❧

Message to the host

Name(s): _____

Date of my/our visit: _____

I/we traveled from: _____

Highlights of my/our stay

_____

_____

_____

Places I / we recommend

_____

_____

_____

_____

Message to the host

_____

_____

_____

Name(s): --

Date of my/our visit: --

I/we traveled from: --

Highlights of my/our stay

Places I / we recommend

Message to the host

Made in the USA
Las Vegas, NV
04 December 2024